• TO _____

• FROM _____

CARS

NAME THE COMPANY

_____ _____ _____ _____

_____ _____ _____ _____

_____ _____ _____ _____

_____ _____ _____ _____

_____ _____ _____ _____

_____ _____ _____ _____

CAR MAKES AND MAKERS

Across

1 _____ Buick - founder Buick Motor Company

4 Fired from The Henry Ford Company ___ ___

6 Bought out of bankruptcy by Henry Ford - ___ Motor Company

8 Henry Ford's only son

9 The Rapp Engine Works - Beyerische Motoren Werke GmbH

14 First gasoline powered motor vehicle - ___ Patent Moorwagen

15 ___ Motor Vehicle Co. of Lansing Michigan founder - Ransom E. ___

19 Named after French Nobleman who founded Detroit

20 Founded by Andre-Gustave _____

21 The Swallow Sidecar Company - became

22 Named after 11 year old _____ Jellinek

Down

2 William C. ___ founder of General Motors

3 _____ - Overland Inc.

5 Changed the 'd' to a 't' to make a more elegant script

7 FIAT (Fabbrica Italiani Automobili ____)

10 The _____ Buggy Company

11 International Motors Company -became

12 Invented the Overhead Valve Engine - David _____

13 Swiss Born race Car Driver - Louis ____

16 Svenska Aeroplanaktiebolaget

17 Auto Avio Costruzioni - became ____

18 Bought the naming rights to Maxwell Motor Company - Walter P. ___

CAR MAKES AND MAKERS

MUSCLE CARS AND THEIR ENGINES

Match The Muscle Car with The Engine

1. '49 Oldsmobile Rocket 88
2. '55 Chrysler C-300
3. '56 Studebaker Golden Hawk
4. '62 Dodge Dart
5. '61 Chevrolet Impala SS
6. '65 Fords
7. '65 Mopars
8. '65 GTO
9. '67 Rambler Marlin
10. '70 Plymouth Duster
11. '70 Rebel Machine
12. '69 Plymouth Road Runner

A. 352 cu in Packard V8
B. 409 cu in V8
C. 427 cu in Thunderbolt V8
D. 383 cu in V8
E. 413 cu in Max Wedge V8
F. 340 cu in V8
G. 331 cu in FirePower V8
H. 343 cu in Typhoon V8
I. 426 cu in Hemi V8
J. 303 cu in V8
K. 389 cu in V8
L. 390 cu in V8

FIND 10
Differences

MUSCLE CAR QUIZ

1. A Muscle Car' was a car
- ❑ with a sophisticated chassis
- ❑ designed for straight line speed
- ❑ a small car with a large displacement engine
- ❑ similar to a European performance car

2. In the 50s and 60s 'Muscle Cars' were called
- ❑ Hot Rods
- ❑ Supercars
- ❑ Speedsters
- ❑ Dragsters

3. 'Muscle Cars' included
- ❑ '65 Pontiac GTO
- ❑ '65 SC/Rambler
- ❑ '56 Studebaker Golden Hawk
- ❑ '55 Chrysler C-300

4. The first 'Muscle Car' was
- ❑ '51 Hudson Hornet
- ❑ '49 Oldsmobile Rocket 88

5. Full-size 'Muscle Cars'
- ❑ '70 Buick Wildcat
- ❑ '70 AMC Rebel
- ❑ '76 AMC Gremlin
- ❑ '67 Mercury Cougar
- ❑ '65 Dodge Polara

MUSCLE CAR QUIZ

6. Not a 'Muscle Car' Designation

- [ ] GS
- [ ] SS
- [ ] RS
- [ ] GSX
- [ ] SC
- [ ] SP
- [ ] R/T
- [ ] RFS

7. Not a 'Muscle Truck'

- [ ] '75 Chevrolet El Camino
- [ ] '75 Ford Ranchero
- [ ] '68 Chevrolet C/K10
- [ ] '74 GMC Sprint
- [ ] '78 Dodge L'il Red Express

8. Pony Car 'Muscle Cars'

- [ ] '69 AMC AMX
- [ ] '70 Dodge Challenger RT
- [ ] '71 AMC Matador Machine
- [ ] '70 Chevrolet Biscayne

9. Mid-size 'Muscle Cars'

- [ ] '73 Chevrolet Bel Air
- [ ] '66 Mercury S-55
- [ ] '73 Plymouth Fury GT
- [ ] '74 Ford Torino

10. Compact 'Muscle Cars'

- [ ] '70 Rebel Machine
- [ ] '70 Buick Skylark
- [ ] '73 Chevy Nova SS
- [ ] '72 Chevrolet Chevelle

MATCHING
CARS IN MOVIES

1. 1960s Batman TV Series

2. James Bond 1977 'The Spy Who Loved Me'

3. 'the Love Bug' 1968

4. 'Ferris Bueller's Day Off' 1986

5. 'Dukes of Hazard' TV 1979

6. 'Smokey and the Bandit 1977

7. 'Back to the Future' 1985

8. 'Bullitt' 1968

9. 'Bullitt' 1968 - The Bad Guys

10. 'Eleanor' Gone in 60 Seconds 2000

11. 'Eleanor - Gone in 60 Seconds 1974

12. 'The Transporter' 2002

13. 'Transporter 2' 2006

14. 'Transporter 4 Refueled' 2015

15. 'The Fast and the Furious' 2001 - Vince's Car

16. 'The Italian Job' 2003

17. 'Thelma and Louise' 1991

18. 'Get Smart' TV Series 1965

19. 'Christine' 1983

20. 'Ghostbusters' 2016

A. 1977 Pontiac Trans Am

B. 1968 Ford Mustang 390 GT

C. 1958 Plymouth Fury

D. 1977 Lotus Esprit

E. 1998 BMW 750iL

F. 1965 Sunbeam Tiger

G. 2012 Audi S8

H. 1967 Shelby Mustang GT500

I. 2003 Mini Cooper

J. 1968 Dodge Charger 440 Magnum

K. 1981 DeLorean DMC-12

L. 1963 Volkswagen Beetle

M. 1973 Mustang Mach 1

N. 1955 Lincoln

O. 2004 Audi A8

P. 1980 Cadillac Fleetwood

Q. 1961 Ferrari 250 GT

R. 1999 Nissan Maxima

S. 1966 Ford Thunderbird

T. 1969 Dodge Charger

WORD FIND
ENGINE WORDS

VISCOSITY	TEN-W-FORTY	ANTIFREEZE
RADIATOR	BEARING	LIFTERS
FAN	CRANKSHAFT	BATTERY
BLOWER	TIMINGBELT	FANBELT
MANIFORLD	EXHAUST	TIMING
GASKET	SPARKPLUG	FUEL
INLINE	V-EIGHT	CARBURETOR
COMBUSTION	HEMI	HYBRID
HORSEPOWER	INJECTION	CAMSHAFT
COMPRESSION	PAN	CYLINDER
OILPAN	TORQUE	BLOCK

Find the words in the
grid on the next page

ENGINE WORDS

```
O K O G T N E Q I A Y X R T B E U Q R O T Y G P
D S U P Q I Q N D C T Y T L E B G N I M I T Z S
C S W K D H A Z O K R Y F Q Z X W U O I Z D C T
V T S K D P T Y F E O R H N J V M H M O L J H N
R V U W L T D P C U F K A J O G P O P R D G P S
H D A T J J R T H P W Q X Y F T Q L O A T Z A P
M I O H L D L B F F N Z U T A M T F Y E Y X N A
Y R E T T A B O Y K E Z K I N R I S V M S X W R
E R R H U N G W H H T Z C C A N A E U P P P B K
K O L A M U A P F C M O R D A G T L E B N A F P
A T D E Z U S W I W N A I M O H Q K Y T M Z H L
O E E W R J K W J O N A W O D S Y E M H O O D U
A R N D D O E W I K T Z F Y K U F W C F H U C G
U U I A R J T T S O B L O C K D F O L D G L F J
C B L J S U H R G C Y L I N D E R G E I H R A
L R N M A E A T J R E R F T V I F P N F U L Z N
M A I D J F H I P G N I R A E B U M T C X F E T
X C R N T T F A H S M A C S C X C E R V J N A I
I V I S C O S I T Y N O I S S E R P M O C U E F
I G Y S C Q Q U I L Y U B S I S F R G R G D Z R
P B C B U W I M A H P A C C P P D A O W N E A E
M O Q C E P E K L H D H B L O W E R J S Z B E E
I V Y D B H R E E B X D Z H O R S E P O W E R Z
F Z F A X P I G U V U E Q L S H T I M I N G C E
```

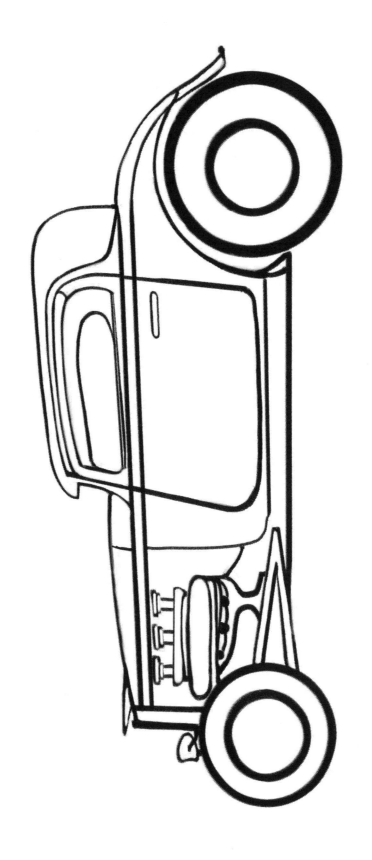

Create Your Own Custom Rod

TIRES AND WHEELS
MATCH the EVENT with the DATE

- ❖ Michelin Tire Company Incorporated
- ❖ The first tubeless tire
- ❖ Henry Ford conveyor built car
- ❖ Benz Motorwagen - First Automotive wheel by Karl Benz (metal tire covered with rubber and filled with air)
- ❖ First Radial Tire
- ❖ The first balloon tire
- ❖ First gasoline powered car
- ❖ First steel welded spoke wheels
- ❖ Industrialized synthetic rubber
- ❖ First vehicle with radial tires
- ❖ First pneumatic rubber car tires Andre and Edouard Michelin
- ❖ First Radial Tire
- ❖ Pneumatic Tire
- ❖ First American made vehicle with Radial tires
- ❖ Run Flat
- ❖ NPT (Non Pneumatic Tire)
- ❖ First wire tension spokes GF Bauer
- ❖ First iron rims

2012
▲
1979
■
1970
■
1949
1948
■
1931
■
1926
■
1923
■
1915
■
1913
■
1903
■
1892
■
1891
■
1889
■
1888
■
1885
■
1845
■
1000 BC

CAR PEOPLE – RACERS AND COLLECTORS

CLUES

1. Millionaire, Talk Show host, Car Collector

2. An actor who raced or a racer who acted?

3. Buyer not a Sellers   4. Rockford at the Grand Prix

5. Plays a Doctor - Owns a racing team

6. America's most trusted newsman

7. Oscar Winner – has a French Connection

8. #23   9. Fashion and Car Art

10. Bean there collected that

11. 'TBE' - Pays for his cars in cash

12. Maybe Kramer helps with the Porsche Collection

13. Who she was

14. Fast and Furious

15. Winning – the most successful celebrity racer in history

16. Actor/Racer – Usually in the Middle

17. The Giant with a Silver Porsche 550 Spyder

CAR PEOPLE – RACERS AND COLLECTORS

1. JYA EOLN _____

2. VSTEE EENUQMC _____

3. TREPE SSRELEL _____

4. MEJAS RARGNE

5. PAKCTRI PYSEMED _____

6. WTAELR ETIRKOCN _____

7. GNEE NCAHAKM _____

8. IVDDA BCHEAKM _____

9. RAPLH AULNER _____

10. ONWRA IATOKNSN _____

11. FOLDY AHRMAYEWTE

12. YRJER SENEIFLD _____

13. UBRCE EJNERN _____

14. PAUL LARWEK _____

15. AULP NMAENW _____

16. KAIFNRE IZMNU _____

17. MAJES NAED _____

CAR PARTS
CROSSWORD
Questions

Across

2 Window ____

5 ABS - Anti-Lock ____ System

7 Charging System - ____

8 Starter ____

9 Wrist Pin

10 Gear Train

13 Voltage ____

14 Fog ____

15 ____ Coil

17 Rocker ___ Cover

20 Battery ____

21 Ignition ____

22 Rev Counter

28 Ball ____

Down

1 Door water - ____

3 Mass Airflow ____

4 Wiring

6 ____ Player

11 Main Pivot in the steering mechanism

12 Turbine-driven forced induction device

16 Floating or Fixed Brake ____

18 Water ____

19 Ensures optimal engine performance

23 Center ___

24 ____ Joint

25 Fuel ____

26 Mileometer

27 ____ Converter

CAR PARTS

CREATE THREE DIFFERENT RACERS

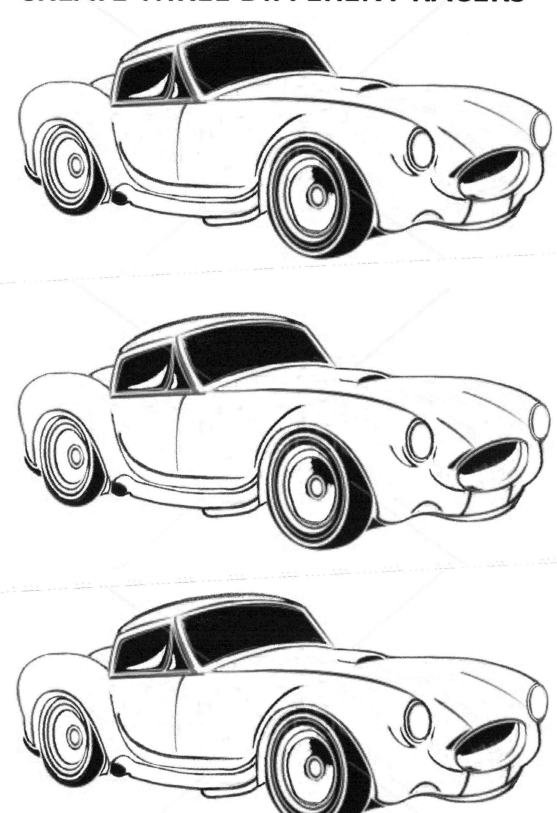

Raceway Trivia

1. Outside Tooele?

- ☐ Daytona Inter. Speedway
- ☐ Road America
- ☐ Utah Motorsports Campus
- ☐ Sebring Inter. Raceway
- ☐ Thunderhill Raceway Park

2. The Cyclone?

- ☐ Daytona Inter. Speedway
- ☐ Road America
- ☐ Utah Motorsports Campus
- ☐ Sebring Inter. Raceway
- ☐ Thunderhill Raceway Park

3. Lake Lloyd?

- ☐ Daytona Inter. Speedway
- ☐ Road America
- ☐ Utah Motorsports Campus
- ☐ Sebring Inter. Raceway
- ☐ Thunderhill Raceway Park

4. 3.56 Mile Loop?

- ☐ Daytona Inter. Speedway
- ☐ Road America
- ☐ Utah Motorsports Campus
- ☐ Sebring Inter. Raceway
- ☐ Thunderhill Raceway Park

5. The BRIC Wreck?

- ☐ Daytona Inter. Speedway
- ☐ Road America
- ☐ Utah Motorsports Campus
- ☐ Sebring Inter. Raceway
- ☐ Thunderhill Raceway Park

6. Scream / Diablo?

- ☐ Daytona Inter. Speedway
- ☐ Road America
- ☐ Utah Motorsports Campus
- ☐ Sebring Inter. Raceway
- ☐ Thunderhill Raceway Park

Raceway Trivia Pg2

7. Florida? (2)

❑ Daytona Inter. Speedway
❑ Road America
❑ Utah Motorsports Campus
❑ Sebring Inter. Raceway
❑ Thunderhill Raceway Park

8. Elkhart Lake?

❑ Daytona Inter. Speedway
❑ Road America
❑ Utah Motorsports Campus
❑ Sebring Inter. Raceway
❑ Thunderhill Raceway Park

9. Halloween 1993?

❑ Daytona Inter. Speedway
❑ Road America
❑ Utah Motorsports Campus
❑ Sebring Inter. Raceway
❑ Thunderhill Raceway Park

10. Longest until 2014?

❑ Daytona Inter. Speedway
❑ Road America
❑ Utah Motorsports Campus
❑ Sebring Inter. Raceway
❑ Thunderhill Raceway Park

11. Near Willows?

❑ Daytona Inter. Speedway
❑ Road America
❑ Utah Motorsports Campus
❑ Sebring Inter. Raceway
❑ Thunderhill Raceway Park

12. Turn 17?

❑ Daytona Inter. Speedway
❑ Road America
❑ Utah Motorsports Campus
❑ Sebring Inter. Raceway
❑ Thunderhill Raceway Park

Raceway Trivia Pg 3

13. Occupies a portion of a functioning airport?

- ☐ Daytona Inter. Speedway
- ☐ Road America
- ☐ Utah Motorsports Campus
- ☐ Sebring Inter. Raceway
- ☐ Thunderhill Raceway Park

16. Wisconsin?

- ☐ Daytona Inter. Speedway
- ☐ Road America
- ☐ Utah Motorsports Campus
- ☐ Sebring Inter. Raceway
- ☐ Thunderhill Raceway Park

14. The Cyclone?

- ☐ Daytona Inter. Speedway
- ☐ Road America
- ☐ Utah Motorsports Campus
- ☐ Sebring Inter. Raceway
- ☐ Thunderhill Raceway Park

17. Speedweeks?

- ☐ Daytona Inter. Speedway
- ☐ Road America
- ☐ Utah Motorsports Campus
- ☐ Sebring Inter. Raceway
- ☐ Thunderhill Raceway Park

15. 101,000 Permanent seats?

- ☐ Daytona Inter. Speedway
- ☐ Road America
- ☐ Utah Motorsports Campus
- ☐ Sebring Inter. Raceway
- ☐ Thunderhill Raceway Park

18. New Year's Eve 1950?

- ☐ Daytona Inter. Speedway
- ☐ Road America
- ☐ Utah Motorsports Campus
- ☐ Sebring Inter. Raceway
- ☐ Thunderhill Raceway Park

Raceway Trivia Pg 4

19. September 1955?

- ❑ Daytona Inter. Speedway
- ❑ Road America
- ❑ Utah Motorsports Campus
- ❑ Sebring Inter. Raceway
- ❑ Thunderhill Raceway Park

20. Longest Auto race in the U.S.?

- ❑ Daytona Inter. Speedway
- ❑ Road America
- ❑ Utah Motorsports Campus
- ❑ Sebring Inter. Raceway
- ❑ Thunderhill Raceway Park

21. Hwy 164?

- ❑ Daytona Inter. Speedway
- ❑ Road America
- ❑ Utah Motorsports Campus
- ❑ Sebring Inter. Raceway
- ❑ Thunderhill Raceway Park

22. Safety Pin?

- ❑ Daytona Inter. Speedway
- ❑ Road America
- ❑ Utah Motorsports Campus
- ❑ Sebring Inter. Raceway
- ❑ Thunderhill Raceway Park

23. Pirelli World Challenge?(3)

- ❑ Daytona Inter. Speedway
- ❑ Road America
- ❑ Utah Motorsports Campus
- ❑ Sebring Inter. Raceway
- ❑ Thunderhill Raceway Park

24. Miller Motorsports Park?

- ❑ Daytona Inter. Speedway
- ❑ Road America
- ❑ Utah Motorsports Campus
- ❑ Sebring Inter. Raceway
- ❑ Thunderhill Raceway Park

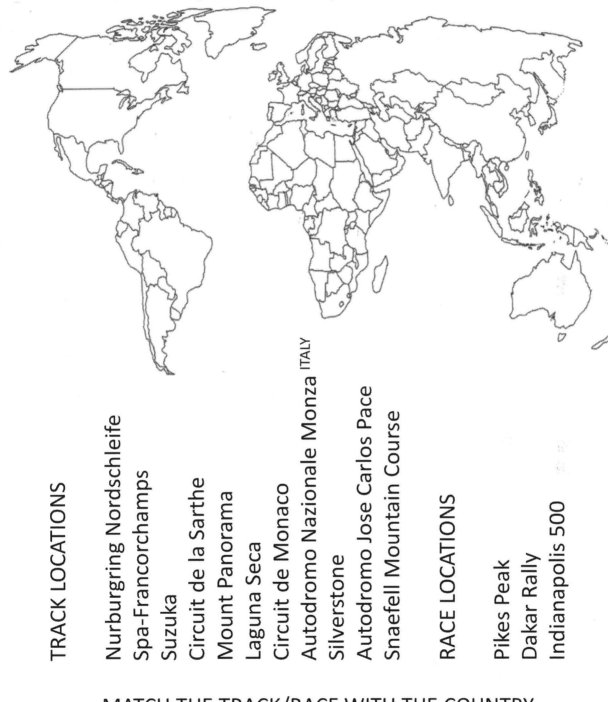

TRACK LOCATIONS

Nurburgring Nordschleife
Spa-Francorchamps
Suzuka
Circuit de la Sarthe
Mount Panorama
Laguna Seca
Circuit de Monaco
Autodromo Nazionale Monza ITALY
Silverstone
Autodromo Jose Carlos Pace
Snaefell Mountain Course

RACE LOCATIONS

Pikes Peak
Dakar Rally
Indianapolis 500

MATCH THE TRACK/RACE WITH THE COUNTRY

Trace / Modify and Color — Create Your Own Custom Ride

Sweden   Czech Republic   Ukraine
Pakistan,   Philippines,   Romania

General Motors

Fiat Chrysler

Volkwagen

Honda

Toyota

Ford

Match the car company with the countries where they build cars – Not parts or engines and not partnerships or licenced agreements

South Korea   Columbia
Hungary, Indonesia, Kazakhstan

United States
Canada
Mexico
France
United kingdom
Germany
Switzerland
Italy
Russia
Bulgaria
Poland
Slovakia
Belgium
India
Austria
Japan
Netherlands
Spain
Portugal
Thailand
South Africa
Brazil
China
Taiwan
Turkey
Romania
Vietnam
Argentina
Venezuela

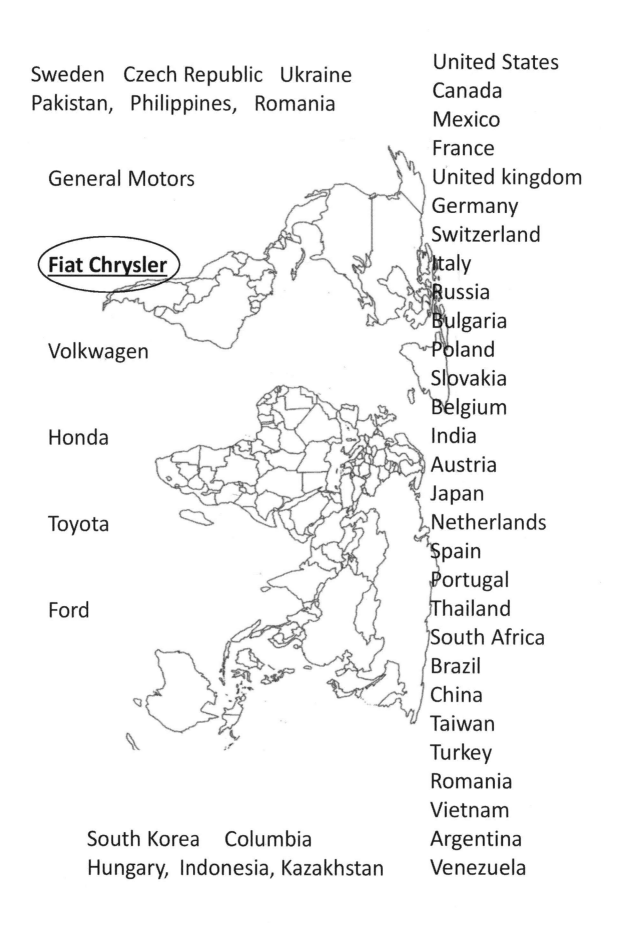

Sweden   Czech Republic   Ukraine
Pakistan, Philippines, Romania

General Motors

Fiat Chrysler

Volkwagen

Honda

Toyota

Ford

South Korea   Columbia
Hungary, Indonesia, Kazakhstan

United States
Canada
Mexico
France
United kingdom
Germany
Switzerland
Italy
Russia
Bulgaria
Poland
Slovakia
Belgium
India
Austria
Japan
Netherlands
Spain
Portugal
Thailand
South Africa
Brazil
China
Taiwan
Turkey
Romania
Vietnam
Argentina
Venezuela

Sweden   Czech Republic   Ukraine
Pakistan,   Philippines,   Romania

General Motors

Fiat Chrysler

Volkwagen

Honda

Toyota

Ford

South Korea   Columbia
Hungary, Indonesia, Kazakhstan

United States
Canada
Mexico
France
United kingdom
Germany
Switzerland
Italy
Russia
Bulgaria
Poland
Slovakia
Belgium
India
Austria
Japan
Netherlands
Spain
Portugal
Thailand
South Africa
Brazil
China
Taiwan
Turkey
Romania
Vietnam
Argentina
Venezuela

Sweden   Czech Republic   Ukraine
Pakistan, Philippines, Romania

General Motors

Fiat Chrysler

Volkwagen

(**Honda**)

Toyota

Ford

South Korea   Columbia
Hungary, Indonesia, Kazakhstan

United States
Canada
Mexico
France
United kingdom
Germany
Switzerland
Italy
Russia
Bulgaria
Poland
Slovakia
Belgium
India
Austria
Japan
Netherlands
Spain
Portugal
Thailand
South Africa
Brazil
China
Taiwan
Turkey
Romania
Vietnam
Argentina
Venezuela

Sweden   Czech Republic   Ukraine
Pakistan, Philippines, Romania

General Motors

Fiat Chrysler

Volkwagen

Honda

Toyota

Ford

South Korea   Columbia
Hungary, Indonesia, Kazakhstan

United States
Canada
Mexico
France
United kingdom
Germany
Switzerland
Italy
Russia
Bulgaria
Poland
Slovakia
Belgium
India
Austria
Japan
Netherlands
Spain
Portugal
Thailand
South Africa
Brazil
China
Taiwan
Turkey
Romania
Vietnam
Argentina
Venezuela

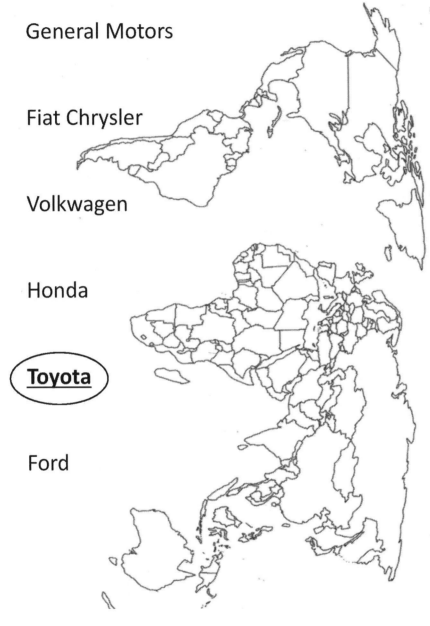

Sweden   Czech Republic   Ukraine
Pakistan, Philippines, Romania

General Motors

Fiat Chrysler

Volkwagen

Honda

Toyota

(Ford)

South Korea   Columbia
Hungary, Indonesia, Kazakhstan

United States
Canada
Mexico
France
United kingdom
Germany
Switzerland
Italy
Russia
Bulgaria
Poland
Slovakia
Belgium
India
Austria
Japan
Netherlands
Spain
Portugal
Thailand
South Africa
Brazil
China
Taiwan
Turkey
Romania
Vietnam
Argentina
Venezuela

Rank the Car Companies by size
(number of Vehicles sold (2015))

RANKING

FORD   –
HYUNDAI   –
NISSAN   –
FIAT CHRYSLER –
PSA   –
MITSUBISHI   –
TATA   –
GM   –
VOLKSWAGEN   –
TOYOTA   –
RENAUT   –
BMW   –
HONDA   –
MAZDA   –

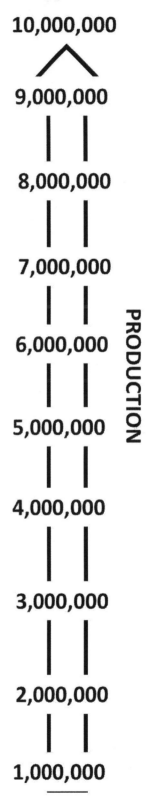

10,000,000

9,000,000

8,000,000

7,000,000

6,000,000

5,000,000

4,000,000

3,000,000

2,000,000

1,000,000

PRODUCTION

FIND THE MATCHING PAIRS

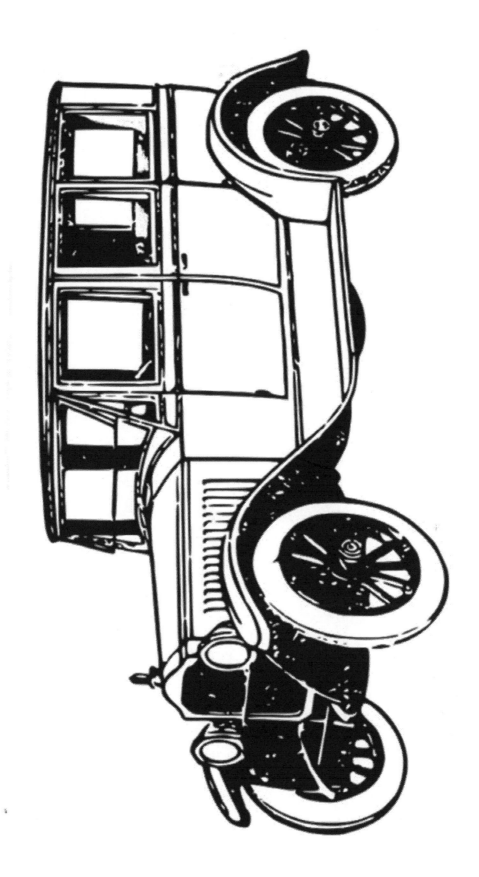

CAR TRIVIA

Down

1 Super____

2 Pontiac GTO - Gran Turismo

3 The first 4 in Oldsmobile 4-4-2

6 A Goat

7 Original Pony Car

9 Kathryn Elizabeth Minner -
from_____

10 little old lady from Pasadena's car

11 Here come the '69 Pontiac GTO

13 AMC Pony Car

14 '68 Mustang vs '68 Charger

15 Advantage of the TF-X - It will

17 Smallest vehicle in the Convoy
(song)

18   Cars look better in the shade

Across

4 Second 4 in Oldsmobile 4-4-2

5 2 in Oldsmobile 4-4-2

8 '32 Ford Hot Rod (2W)

12 Hand built and free of Hot Rod Characteristics
(2W)

16 The Love Bug

19 Shelby

CAR TRIVIA

**FIND THE 8
DIFFERENCES**

WHAT DO YOU THINK THE WORLD'S MOST EXPENSIVE CARS COST?

CAR

$$$$ COST $$$$

▲

$8 MILLION

KOENIGSEGG CCXR Trevita

LAMBORGHINI VENENO

W MOTORS LYKAN HYPERSPORT

Zenvo TS1 GT

KOENIGSEGG REGERA

$5 MILLION

MERCEDES-BENZ MAYBACH EXELERO

Ruf CTR – PORSCH 911

$4 MILLION

PAGANI HUAYRA BC

BUGATTI VEYRON (Limited Edition)

FERRARI PININFORINA SERGIO

$3 MILLION

FERRARI F60 AMERICA

BUGATTI CHIRON

KOENIGSEGG ONE:1

$2 MILLION

ASTON MARTIN VALKYRIE

ROLLS-ROYCE PHANTOM SERENITY

ASTON MARTIN One-77

$1 MILLION

ANSWERS

NAME THE COMPANY

Volvo

Vauxhall

Mahindra

Corvette

Tata

Subaru

Honda

Buick

Wiesmann

Skoda

Great Wall

Ariel

Zaz

Maybach

Dodge

Bentley

Scania

Morgan

Chrysler

Aston Martin

Suzuki

Peugeot

Chevrolet

Acura

CAR MAKES AND MAKERS

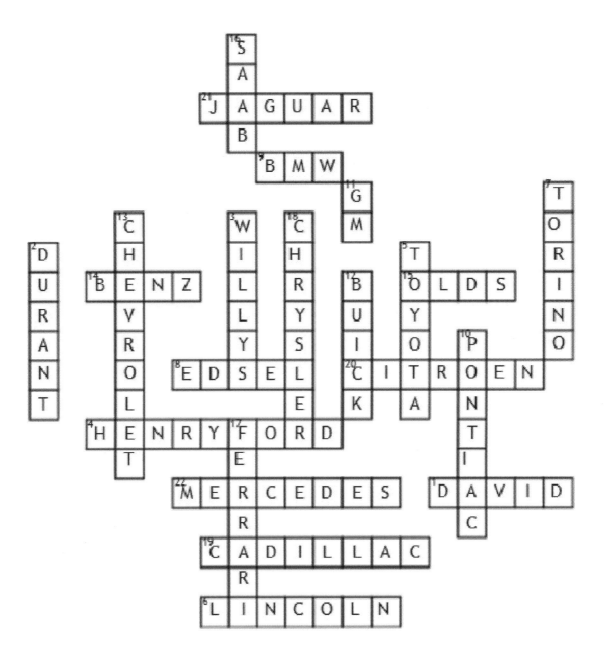

CAR MAKES AND MAKERS

Across

1. _____ Buick - founder Buick Motor Company

4. Fired from The Henry Ford Company ___ ___

6. Bought out of bankruptcy by Henry Ford - ____ Motor Company

8. Henry Ford's only son

9. The Rapp Engine Works - Beyerische Motoren Werke GmbH

14. First gasoline powered motor vehicle - ____ Patent Moorwagen

15. ____ Motor Vehicle Co. of Lansing Michigan founder - Ransom E. ___

19. Named after French Nobleman who founded Detroit

20. Founded by Andre-Gustave _____

21. The Swallow Sidecar Company - became

22. Named after 11 year old _____ Jellinek

Down

2. William C. ____ founder of General Motors

3. _____ - Overland Inc.

5. Changed the 'd' to a 't' to make a more elegant script

7. FIAT (Fabbrica Italiani Automobili _____)

10. The _____ Buggy Company

11. International Motors Company - became

12. Invented the Overhead Valve Engine - David _____

13. Swiss Born race Car Driver - Louis _____

16. Svenska Aeroplanaktiebolaget

17. Auto Avio Costruzioni - became _____

18. Bought the naming rights to Maxwell Motor Company - Walter P. ____

MUSCLE CARS AND THEIR ENGINES

1. '49 Oldsmobile Rocket 88 **J**   A. 352 cu in Packard V8

2. '55 Chrysler C-300 **G**   B. 409 cu in V8

3. '56 Studebaker Golden Hawk **A**C. 427 cu in Thunderbolt V8

4. '62 Dodge Dart **E**   D. 383 cu in V8

5. '61 Chevrolet Impala SS **B**   E. 413 cu in Max Wedge V8

6. '65 Fords **C**   F. 340 cu in V8

7. '65 Mopars **I**   G. 331 cu in FirePower V8

8. '65 GTO **K**   H. 343 cu in Typhoon V8

9. '67 Rambler Marlin **H**   I. 426 cu in Hemi V8

10. '70 Plymouth Duster **F**   J. 303 cu in V8

11. '70 Rebel Machine **L**   K. 389 cu in V8

12. '69 Plymouth Road Runner **D** L. 390 cu in V8

FIND 10
Differences

1. A Muscle Car' was a car
   with a sophisticated chassis
✓ designed for straight line speed
✓ a small car with a large displacement engine
   similar to a European performance car

2. In the 50s and 60s 'Muscle Cars' were called
   Hot Rods
✓ Supercars
   Speedsters
   Dragsters

3. 'Muscle Cars' included

✓ '65 Pontiac GTO
✓ '65 SC/Rambler
✓ '56 Studebaker Golden Hawk
✓ '55 Chrysler C-300

4. The first 'Muscle Car' was
   '51 Hudson Hornet
✓ '49 Oldsmobile Rocket 88

5. Full-size 'Muscle Cars'

✓ '70 Buick Wildcat
❑ '70 AMC Rebel
❑ '76 AMC Gremlin
❑ '67 Mercury Cougar
✓ '65 Dodge Polara

MUSCLE

CAR

QUIZ

6. Not a 'Muscle Car' Designation

GS SS

RS

GSX

SC

SP

R/T

✓ RFS

7. Not a 'Muscle Truck'

'75 Chevrolet El Camino

'75 Ford Ranchero

✓ '68 Chevrolet C/K10

'74 GMC Sprint

'78 Dodge L'il Red Express

MUSCLE CAR QUIZ

8. Pony Car 'Muscle Cars'

✓ '69 AMC AMX

✓ '70 Dodge Challenger RT

❏ '71 AMC Matador Machine

❏ '70 Chevrolet Biscayne

9. Mid-size 'Muscle Cars'

❏ '73 Chevrolet Bel Air

❏ '66 Mercury S-55

❏ '73 Plymouth Fury GT

✓ '74 Ford Torino

10. Compact 'Muscle Cars'

❏ '70 Rebel Machine

❏ '70 Buick Skylark

✓ '73 Chevy Nova SS

❏ '72 Chevrolet Chevelle

ANSWERS
CARS IN MOVIES

1. 1960s Batman TV Series
2. James Bond 1977 'The Spy Who Loved Me'
3. 'the Love Bug' 1968
4. 'Ferris Bueller's Day Off' 1986
5. 'Dukes of Hazard' TV 1979
6. 'Smokey and the Bandit 1977
7. 'Back to the Future' 1985
8. 'Bullitt' 1968 B
9. 'Bullitt' 1968 - The Bad Guys
10. 'Eleanor' Gone in 60 Seconds 2000
11. 'Eleanor - Gone in 60 Seconds 1974
12. 'The Transporter' 2002
13. 'Transporter2' 2006
14. 'Transporter4 Refueled' 2015
15. 'The Fast and the Furious' 2001 - Vince's Car
16. 'The Italian Job' 2003
17. 'Thelma and Louise' 1991
18. 'Get Smart' TV Series 1965
19. 'Christine' 1983
20. 'Ghostbusters' 2016

N. 1955 Lincoln
D. 1977 Lotus Esprit
L. 1963 Volkswagen Beetle
Q. 1961 Ferrari 250 GT
T. 1969 Dodge Charger
A. 1977 Pontiac Trans Am
K. 1981 DeLorean DMC-12
B. 1968 Ford Mustang 390 GT
J. 1968 Charger 440 Magnum
H. 1967 Shelby Mustang GT500
M. 1973 Mustang Mach 1
E. 1998 BMW 750iL
O. 2004 Audi A8
G. 2012 Audi S8
R. 1999 Nissan Maxima
I. 2003 Mini Cooper
S. 1966 Ford Thunderbird
F. 1965 Sunbeam Tiger
C. 1958 Plymouth Fury
P. 1980 Cadillac Fleetwood

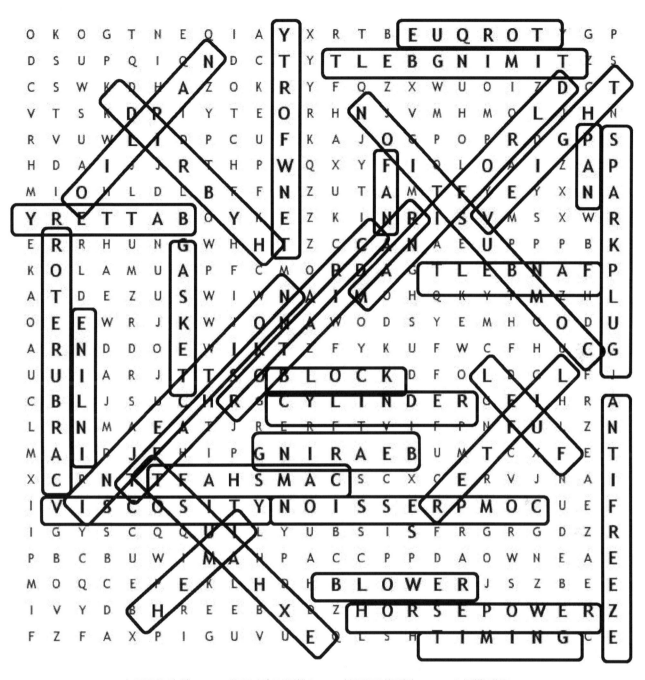

VISCOSITY   TEN-W-FORTY   ANTIFREEZE   RADIATOR

BEARING   LIFTERS   FAN   CRANKSHAFT

BATTERY   BLOWER   TIMINGBELT   FANBELT

MANIFORLD   EXHAUST   TIMING   GASKET

SPARKPLUG   FUEL   INLINE   V-EIGHT

CARBURETOR   COMBUSTION   HEMI   HYBRID

HORSEPOWER   INJECTION   CAMSHAFT   COMPRESSION

PAN   CYLINDER   OILPAN   TORQUE

BLOCK

TIRES AND WHEELS
MATCH the EVENT with the DATE

- Michelin Tire Company Incorporated **1889**
- The tubeless tire - **1903**
- Henry Ford conveyor built car - **1913**
- Benz Motorwagen - First Automotive wheel by Karl Benz (metal tire covered with rubber and filled with air) - **1885**
- First Radial Tire **1915**
- The balloon tire - **1923**
- First gasoline powered car - **1888**
- Steel welded spoke wheels - **1926-27**
- Industrialized synthetic rubber - **1931**
- First vehicle with radial tires - **1948**
- First pneumatic rubber car tires Andre and Edouard Michelin - **1891**
- Radial Tire - **1949**
- Pneumatic Tire - **1845**
- First American made vehicle with Radial tires - **1970**
- Run Flat - **1979**
- NPT (Non Pneumatic Tire) - **2012**
- First wire tension spokes GF Bauer - **1892**
- First iron rims (On Celtic Chariots) **1000 BC**

2012
▲
1979
■
1970
■
1949
1948
■
1931
■
1926
■
1923
■
1915
■
1913
■
1903
1892
■
1891
■
1889
■
1888
■
1885
■
1845
■
1000 BC

CAR PEOPLE - Racers and Collectors

1. JYAEOLN — Jay Leno
2. VSTEE EENUQMC — Steve McQueen
3. TREPE SSRELEL — Peter Sellers
4. MEJAS RARGNE — James Garner
5. PAKCTRIPYSEMED — Patrick Dempsey
6. WTAELRETIRKOCN — Walter Cronkite
7. GNEE NCAHAKM — Gene Hackman
8. IVDDA BCHEAKM — David Beckham
9. RAPLH AULNER — Ralph Lauren
10. ONWRA IATOKNSN — Rowan Atkinson
11. FOLDY AHRMAYEWTE — Floyd Mayweather
12. YRJER SENEIFLD — Jerry Seinfeld
13. UBRCE EJNERN — Bruce Jenner
14. PAULLARWEK — Paul Walker
15. AULP NMAENW — Paul Newman
16. KAIFNRE IZMNU — Frankie Muniz
17. MAJES NAED — James Dean

CAR PARTS

Raceway Trivia - ANSWERS

1. Outside Tooele?

✓ Utah Motorsports Campus
-LOCATION

2. The Cyclone?

✓ Thunderhill Raceway Park
-TURN

3. Lake Lloyd?

✓ Daytona Inter. Speedway

4. 3.56 Mile Loop?

✓ Daytona Inter. Speedway

5. The BRIC Wreck?

✓ Road America
-FAMOUS CRASH

6. Scream / Diablo?

✓ Utah Motorsports Campus
-TURNS

7. Florida?

✓ Daytona Inter. Speedway
✓ Sebring Inter. Raceway

8. Elkhart Lake?

✓ Road America

9. Halloween 1993?

✓ Thunderhill Raceway Park
-FIRST RACE

10. Longest until 2014?

✓ Utah Motorsports Campus
Passed by Thunderhill

11. Near Willows?

✓ Thunderhill Raceway Park

12. Turn 17?

✓ Sebring Inter. Raceway
-TURN

Raceway Trivia – ANSWERS Pg 2

13. Occupies a portion of a functioning airport?

✓ Sebring Inter. Raceway

14. The Cyclone?

✓ Thunderhill Raceway Park - TURN

15. 101,000 Permanent seats?

✓ Daytona Inter. Speedway

16. Wisconsin?

✓ Road America

17. Speedweeks?

✓ Daytona Inter. Speedway JANUARY-FEBRUARY

18. New Year's Eve 1950?

✓ Sebring Inter. Raceway FIRST RACE

19. September 1955?

✓ Road America

20. Longest Auto race in the U.S.?

✓ Thunderhill Raceway Park - 24 HRS AT THUNDERHILL

21. Hwy 164?

✓ Thunderhill Raceway Park

22. Safety Pin?

✓ Sebring Inter. Raceway -TURNS

23. Pirelli World Challenge?

✓ Road America
✓ Utah Motorsports Campus
✓ Sebring Inter. Raceway

24. Miller Motorsports Park?

✓ Utah Motorsports Campus -WAS

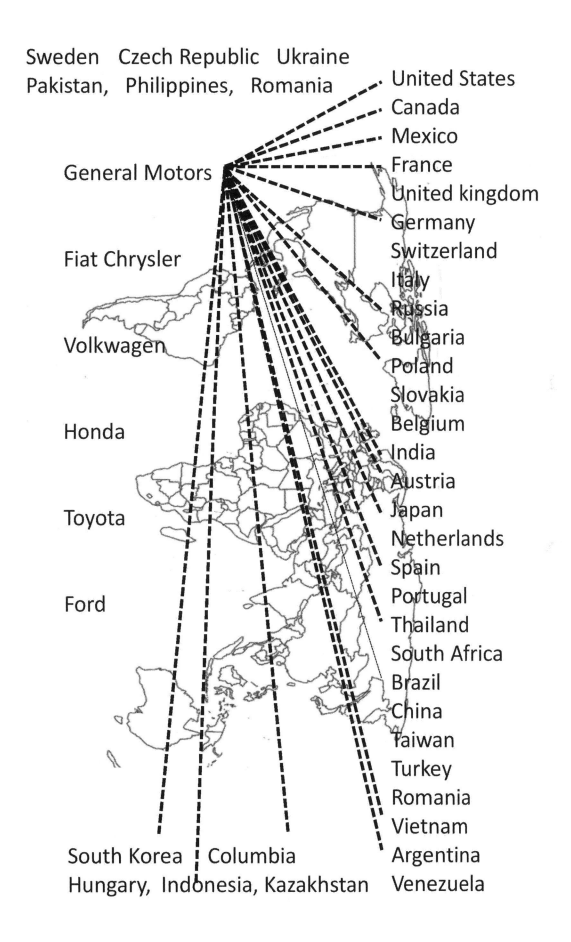

Sweden   Czech Republic   Ukraine
Pakistan,   Philippines,   Romania

General Motors

Fiat Chrysler

Volkwagen

Honda

Toyota

Ford

South Korea   Columbia
Hungary, Indonesia, Kazakhstan

United States
Canada
Mexico
France
United kingdom
Germany
Switzerland
Italy
Russia
Bulgaria
Poland
Slovakia
Belgium
India
Austria
Japan
Netherlands
Spain
Portugal
Thailand
South Africa
Brazil
China
Taiwan
Turkey
Romania
Vietnam
Argentina
Venezuela

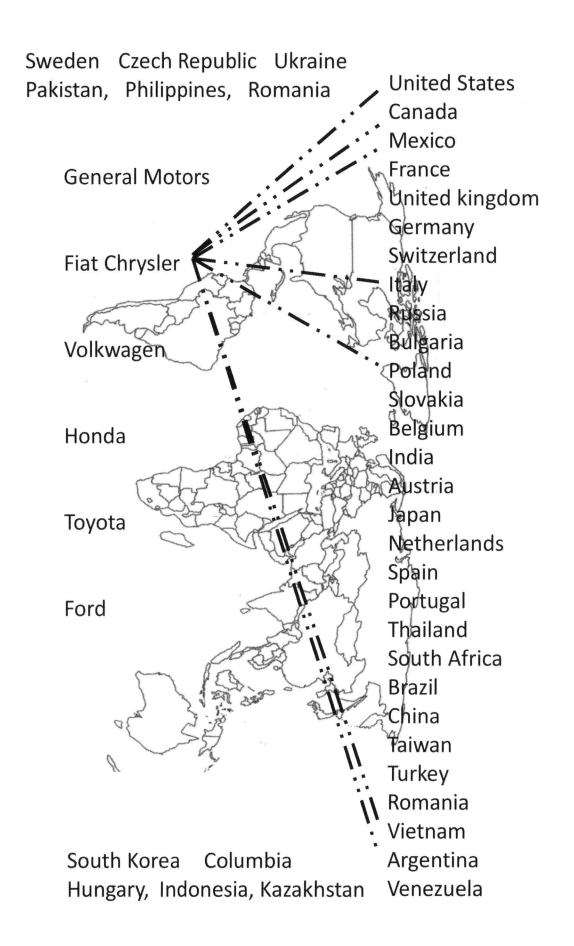

Sweden   Czech Republic   Ukraine
Pakistan,   Philippines,   Romania

United States
Canada
Mexico
France

General Motors

United kingdom
Germany
Switzerland
Italy

Fiat Chrysler

Russia
Bulgaria
Poland
Slovakia

Volkwagen

Belgium
India
Austria

Honda

Japan
Netherlands
Spain

Toyota

Portugal
Thailand
South Africa

Ford

Brazil
China
Taiwan
Turkey
Romania
Vietnam

South Korea   Columbia
Hungary, Indonesia, Kazakhstan

Argentina
Venezuela

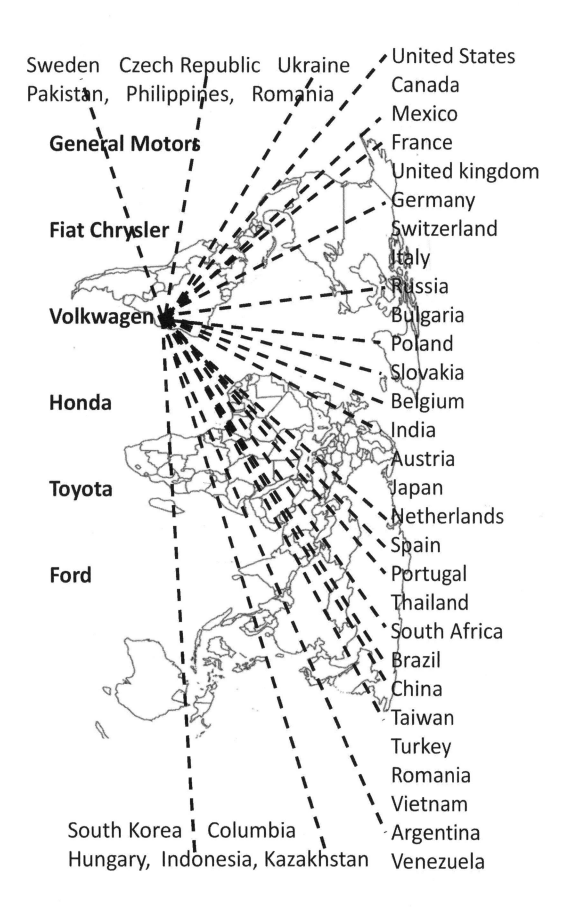

Sweden   Czech Republic   Ukraine   United States
Pakistan, Philippines, Romania   Canada
                                       Mexico
General Motors   France
                                       United kingdom
                                       Germany
Fiat Chrysler   Switzerland
                                       Italy
                                       Russia
                                       Bulgaria
Volkwagen   Poland
                                       Slovakia
                                       Belgium
                                       India
Honda   Austria
                                       Japan
                                       Netherlands
Toyota   Spain
                                       Portugal
                                       Thailand
Ford   South Africa
                                       Brazil
                                       China
                                       Taiwan
                                       Turkey
                                       Romania
                                       Vietnam
South Korea   Columbia   Argentina
Hungary, Indonesia, Kazakhstan   Venezuela

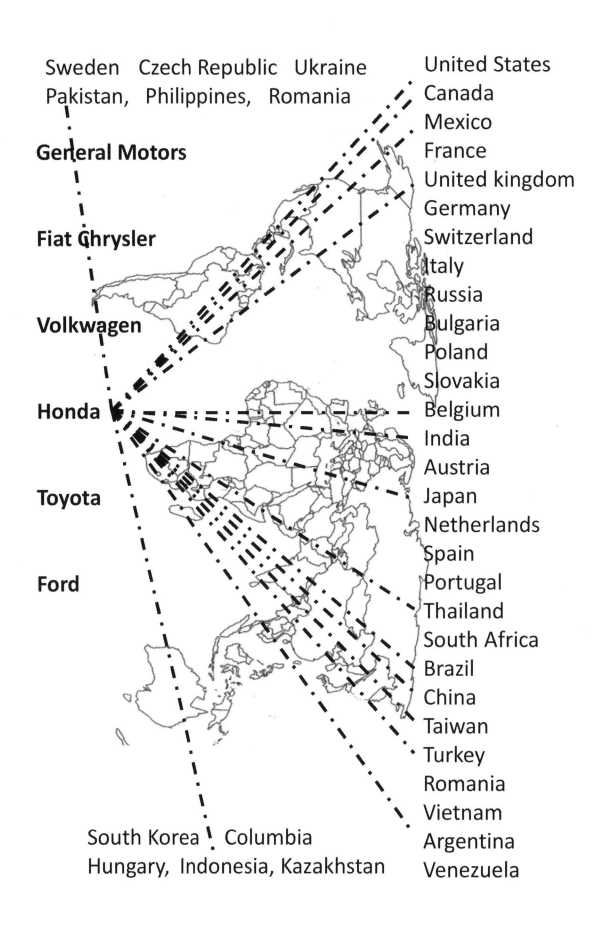

Sweden   Czech Republic   Ukraine   United States
Pakistan, Philippines, Romania   Canada
                                      Mexico
General Motors   France
                                      United kingdom
                                      Germany
Fiat Chrysler   Switzerland
                                      Italy
                                      Russia
Volkwagen   Bulgaria
                                      Poland
                                      Slovakia
Honda   Belgium
                                      India
                                      Austria
                                      Japan
Toyota   Netherlands
                                      Spain
                                      Portugal
Ford   Thailand
                                      South Africa
                                      Brazil
                                      China
                                      Taiwan
                                      Turkey
                                      Romania
                                      Vietnam
South Korea   Columbia   Argentina
Hungary, Indonesia, Kazakhstan   Venezuela

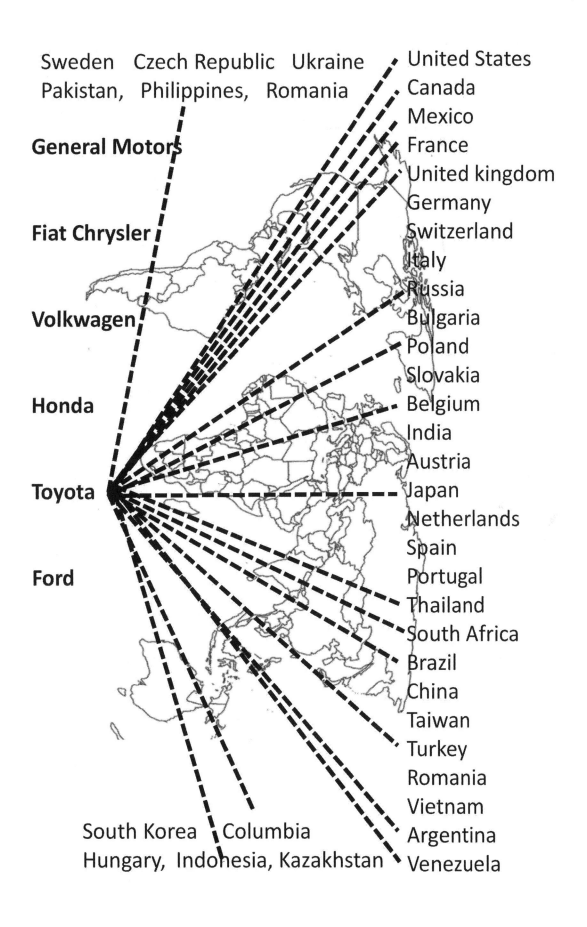

Sweden   Czech Republic   Ukraine   United States
Pakistan,   Philippines,   Romania   Canada
                                      Mexico
General Motors   France
                                      United kingdom
                                      Germany
Fiat Chrysler   Switzerland
                                      Italy
                                      Russia
Volkwagen   Bulgaria
                                      Poland
                                      Slovakia
Honda   Belgium
                                      India
                                      Austria
Toyota   Japan
                                      Netherlands
                                      Spain
Ford   Portugal
                                      Thailand
                                      South Africa
                                      Brazil
                                      China
                                      Taiwan
                                      Turkey
                                      Romania
                                      Vietnam
South Korea   Columbia   Argentina
Hungary,   Indonesia,   Kazakhstan   Venezuela

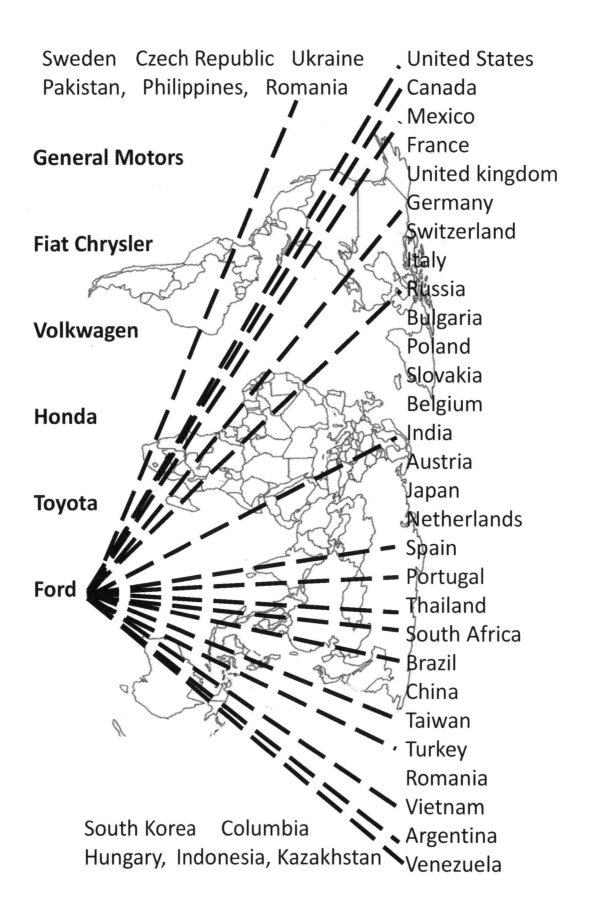

Sweden   Czech Republic   Ukraine   United States
Pakistan,   Philippines,   Romania   Canada
                                        Mexico
General Motors   France
                                        United kingdom
                                        Germany
                                        Switzerland
Fiat Chrysler   Italy
                                        Russia
                                        Bulgaria
                                        Poland
Volkwagen   Slovakia
                                        Belgium
                                        India
Honda   Austria
                                        Japan
                                        Netherlands
Toyota   Spain
                                        Portugal
                                        Thailand
Ford   South Africa
                                        Brazil
                                        China
                                        Taiwan
                                        Turkey
                                        Romania
                                        Vietnam
South Korea   Columbia   Argentina
Hungary, Indonesia, Kazakhstan   Venezuela

Rank the Car Companies by size (number of Vehicles sold (2015))

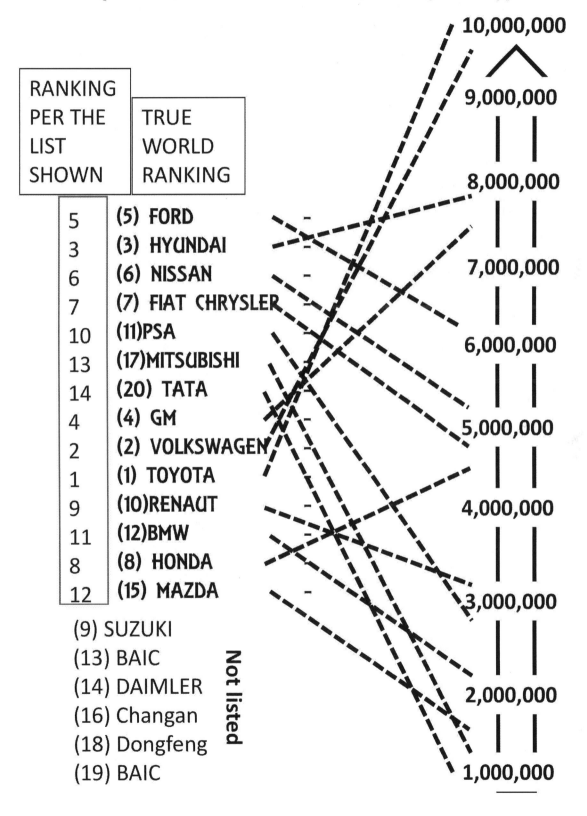

RANKING PER THE LIST SHOWN	TRUE WORLD RANKING
5	(5) FORD
3	(3) HYUNDAI
6	(6) NISSAN
7	(7) FIAT CHRYSLER
10	(11) PSA
13	(17) MITSUBISHI
14	(20) TATA
4	(4) GM
2	(2) VOLKSWAGEN
1	(1) TOYOTA
9	(10) RENAUT
11	(12) BMW
8	(8) HONDA
12	(15) MAZDA

(9) SUZUKI
(13) BAIC
(14) DAIMLER
(16) Changan
(18) Dongfeng
(19) BAIC

Not listed

10,000,000
9,000,000
8,000,000
7,000,000
6,000,000
5,000,000
4,000,000
3,000,000
2,000,000
1,000,000

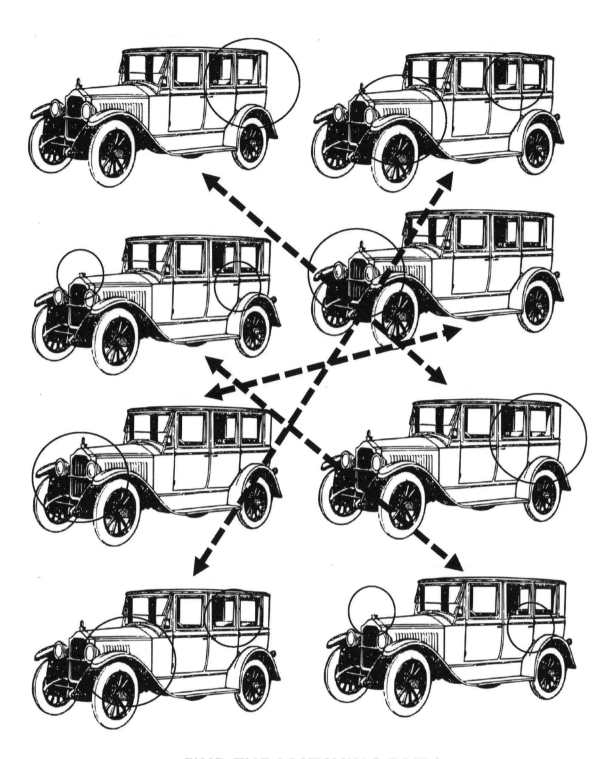

FIND THE MATCHING PAIRS

CAR TRIVIA

Down

1. Super_____
2. Pontiac GTO - Gran Turismo
3. The first 4 in Oldsmobile 4-4-2
6. A Goat
7. Original Pony Car
9. Kathryn Elizabeth Minner - from_____
10. little old lady from Pasadena's car
11. Here come the '69 Pontiac GTO
13. AMC Pony Car
14. '68 Mustang vs '68 Charger
15. Advantage of the TF-X - It will

Across

4. Second 4 in Oldsmobile 4-4-2
5. 2 in Oldsmobile 4-4-2
8. '32 Ford Hot Rod (2W)
12. Hand built and free of Hot Rod Characteristics (2W)
16. The Love Bug
19. Shelby

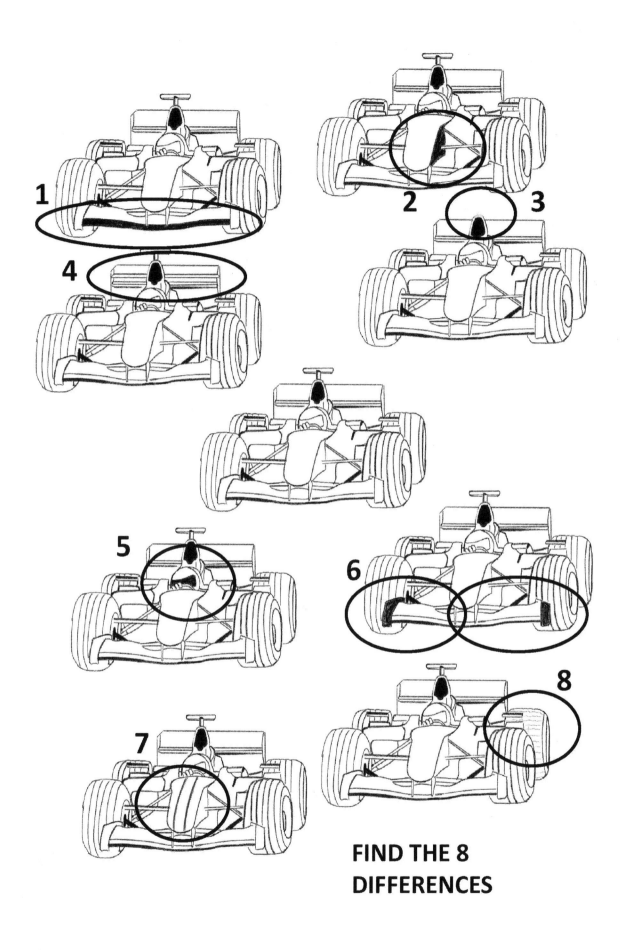

FIND THE 8 DIFFERENCES

WHAT DO YOU THINK THE WORLD'S MOST EXPENSIVE CARS COST?

CAR $$$$ COST $$$$

                                                    ⌃
                                            $8 MILLION
MERCEDES-BENZ MAYBACH EXELERO ($8 M)

KOENIGSEGG CCXR Trevita ($4.8 M)

LAMBORGHINI VENENO ($4.5 M)

W MOTORS LYKAN HYPERSPORT ($3.4 M)

BUGATTI VEYRON (Limited Edition) ($3.4 M) $5 MILLION

FERRARI PININFORINA SERGIO ($3 M)

ASTON MARTIN VALKYRIE ($3 M)

PAGANI HUAYRA BC ($2.6 M) $4 MILLION

FERRARI F60 AMERICA ($2.5 M)   **FOR POOR PEOPLE**

BUGATTI CHIRON ($2.5 M) $3 MILLION

KOENIGSEGG REGERA ($2 M)

KOENIGSEGG ONE:1 ($ 2 M)

ASTON MARTIN One-77 ($1.4 M) $2 MILLION

Zenvo TS1 GT ($1.2 M)

ROLLS-ROYCE PHANTOM SERENITY ($1.1 M)

Ruf CTR – PORSCH 911 ($790,000) $1 MILLION

Made in United States
Orlando, FL
20 April 2022